Touching the Hem

Touching the Hem

Encounters with Jesus
by those who knew him

Jeannine Davies

TOUCHING THE HEM
Encounters with Jesus by those who knew him

© 2003 Jeannine Davies
Original edition published in English under the title TOUCHING THE HEM by Kevin Meyhew Ltd, Buxhall, England.

This edition published in 2020 by Fortress Press. All rights reserved. Except for brief quotations in critical articles or reviews, no part of this book may be reproduced in any manner without prior written permission from the publisher. Email copyright@augsburgfortress.org or write to Permissions, Fortress Press, PO Box 1209, Minneapolis, MN 55440-1209.

Cover image: © iStock 2020: Statue of one of the fathers of botany: Theophrastus stock photo by udokant

Cover design: Emily Drake

Print ISBN: 978-1-5064-6037-6

Contents

Introduction	vii
The Woman with the Haemorrhage	1
'I Am the Potter, You Are the Clay'	3
Stabilisers	5
Legion, the Gerasene Demoniac	7
In Heaven	9
Jesus Walks on the Water	11
Mary Magdalene at the Open Tomb	13
My Cross	15
Zacchaeus	17
Jesus Turns Water into Wine	19
Bartimaeus, the Blind Man	21
Suffer Little Children to Come unto Me	23
The Woman at the Well	25
Trust	27
Jesus Heals a Paralytic	28
A King's Journey	30
Doors	32
God's Promise	34
The Man Born Blind	35
Simeon	37
Jairus' Daughter	39
It's All Right	41
Malchus, the High Priest's Slave and Soldier	43
Mary, the Mother of Jesus	45

CONTENTS

I Am the Good Shepherd	47
Changes	48
'The Holy Spirit that Has Been Given to Us'	49
The Shepherd's Tale	51
The Widow's Mite	53
The Man at the Pool	55
Simon the Pharisee	57
The Crippled Woman	59
Jesus Heals the Deaf Mute	61
Barabbas	64
The Ten Lepers	66
The Field of Corn	69
Simon	71
Zebedee	73
The Raising of the Widow's Son	75
The River of Life	77
I Am the Vine, You Are the Branches	79
The Baptism of Jesus	80
Jesus Heals a Leper	82
The Road to Emmaus	84
The Centurion and His Servant	86
Jesus Feeds the Five Thousand	88
Judas Iscariot	90
Martha and Mary	92
Mary Magdalene	94
Jesus Washes the Disciples' Feet	96
Jesus Appears to the Disciples	98
Return of the Prodigal Son	100

Introduction

It all began when I attended a series of four weekly meditations led by our vicar. I loved the peace of meditating, and happily attended the next series – and the next. During the times of quiet, we were encouraged to think, pray, draw, or even sleep. I wrote. Plucking up the courage, I read my writings to a few friends who encouraged me to send them to Kevin Mayhew – and so, this book was born.

My immense thanks go to Hazel Langley, who not only heard every piece in this book but also spent hours checking my work for errors, and she has prayed and supported me spiritually throughout. My thanks also go to Joan Wearn for listening to these meditations, often in the evening, standing outside church in the winter chill! Joan's eagerness to hear more encouraged me tremendously; and to Pam Ritchie and Lynn Cruttenden, whose prayers, wisdom and companionship I value greatly.

I am indebted to Sarah Chapman, my (then) vicar, for preparing and introducing the meditative sessions and for putting my feet firmly back on the path to Jesus. Clare Gibson was brave enough to test the waters with one or two of these pieces in her house group and she, too, encouraged me to go to print – to you both, thank you.

Thanks too to my family for having faith in me and for their love, patience and support. My daughters, Sharon, Carole and Sophie, have been of immense help, and my husband,

INTRODUCTION

David, and my son, Richard, have remained stoically tolerant and loving throughout.

Finally, dear reader, may I suggest that you do not read too many of these meditations at once. Take it slowly, let the words and meaning sink in – listen to God. I hope your heart is touched, as mine was as I wrote these words.

Jeannine Davies

The Woman with the Haemorrhage
Mark 5:22-43

Now what? Stay or run? Proclaim or keep mum? Speak up and be done with it. The *fear!* Just healed, better at last – two minutes into no-bleed time and it's own-up time . . . what if he 'undoes' the healing?

Lord Jesus, I'm sorry I went behind your back, but to come from the front seemed too much – too much to ask for, too much of a chance – just . . . too much!

And then I saw your face – and, suddenly, I knew it was all right. I could tell you why. Why I did it backwards. And yet . . . it was forwards, after all. You felt my presence anyway, you *knew* – you understood.

Your eyes . . . so kind, so . . . full of love, so . . . you made me feel precious; special, whole.

The Reply

'Go out and proclaim. Tell it again and again and again – just like the birds this evening, in their goodnight call. Go out and tell my people all.'

A Prayer

Had it been me, I would have done the same as she – touched your cloak. I bet she was afraid! Scared

of being found out. She, an untouchable, had *touched* you . . . and was *healed!*

Lord Jesus, it's hard to imagine that you could look on me with so much love, yet you *do*. Thank you for loving me, for seeing something precious and special in me. Help me to spread the wonder of your love to others today. Amen.

'I Am the Potter, You Are the Clay'
Isaiah 64:8

I can see Chris's hands on the clay, and your hands are over hers . . . are you guiding her hands, Lord?

'No, child. My hands are on the clay and Chris's hands are over mine. You see, if my hands were over hers, she might feel pushed – forced to take a direction she doesn't want. With Chris's hands over mine, she can follow each movement as I mould and shape the pot. She can feel my fingers and follow them as they move. If it gets too much for her, she can let go for a while – it's all right to do that, I will still have my hands wrapped about her.

'Then, when the pot is complete, you'll see the shape of my hands indented into the sides. That's to remind you that I live *in* you – and you in me. And, just as I remain invisible within you, so my indented hands on the pot can become invisible; hidden by other hands covering it – but the indent will always be there and you will see, as the covers are removed, that I have had a hand in the shaping of your life.'

'So, Lord, it doesn't matter if the pot is a bit wonky, you've designed it that way – designed us with our own wonkiness – for your purposes!'

'Child, yes. Remember that no one is perfect and that not one of you is the same. I love you as you are . . . yet the pot you are now will not be the end result – trust in me, for I am holding you in my hands.'

A Prayer

Lord Jesus, thank you for loving me as I am, thank you for my own wonkiness. Please mould me and prepare me to be always ready for your use: pliable, ready for change; solid, ready to withstand forces within and without; and steady – steady and ready for you, Lord. Amen.

Stabilisers

My child, I know. I can see your fear and distress at losing the one who has been guiding you, she has been in your life for many years and has been your prop, your mentor and friend.

But you see, child, she must move on now. I have need of her elsewhere. I have other souls who are just as you used to be. They need to be freed of their miseries too.

Trust in me, you can look to *me* for guidance now. Over the years, you have learned how to do that. You can find me now – wherever you are; you know that I am always with you. Your faith has grown.

Child, how does a loving parent teach his child to ride a bicycle? He places stabilisers on each side of the wheel to keep his precious little one safe. I have done the same with you. There comes a time, however, when a parent knows that the child is ready for the stabilisers to be removed and is competent enough to ride without them. My precious one, does a loving parent then leave his child to wobble alone? No, he holds on to the saddle until he knows his child has the balance needed to continue on his or her own.

My child, you *are* ready to go on alone now; I know you feel insecure, scared and alone, but you *can* do it and I will be holding you, just as I have always held you. I will continue to guide you, have faith in me and follow me – I am taking you in a different direction; one where your stabilisers would eventually hinder your progress. I love you. Trust in me; you are mine and I am holding you firmly.

A Prayer

Hold me as I wobble, Lord, hold me tightly. Let me feel your arms wrapped around me – I'm scared! Yet, I know you love me; you will not let me fall. Lord, show me your new direction, I'm ready to go where you lead – I love you. Amen.

Legion, the Gerasene Demoniac
Mark 5:1-13

What did he think he was doing, coming that close to me? Didn't he know I was mad? He must have known; he spoke those words out loud – something to do with demons leaving my body. I shouted at him, 'What do you want with me, Jesus, Son of the Most High God?' Didn't he *know* I could have killed him? Couldn't he see the danger – as he came so close?

I was scared, I can tell you. Scared I'd hit this man with the gentle voice . . . but he just stood there, in front of me; he never even flinched. Everyone else had backed well away – who could blame them? – but not Jesus. He seemed unafraid – happy, even, to be with me. I felt his love for me – *me* – he loved *me*.

Someone mentioned the swine on the hill, I didn't quite grasp what was said, but I saw them running; I felt I was there, with them, running and screaming – out of control – I opened my mouth to scream with them, recognising the inner screaming inside my head . . . but not a sound came out . . . nothing. My voice was silent.

I turned my eyes to Jesus. He was watching me . . . looking at me with such tenderness . . . I was struck still. I kept watching his face – so calm, so gentle. The more I watched, the more clear my head became. He smiled at me and I knew he'd healed me.

It took me a while to get used to my new self. I mean, what does a man *do* after years of living among the tombstones? Yet, look at me now . . . in my right mind, clothed and sitting here with you all – and *you* sitting with *me*. I have come to my senses. I *am* telling it truthfully – it's all I can do for Jesus – tell it with truth.

Oh, how I wanted to go with him, to follow him, to learn and be a part of him. I asked if I could follow – but he said, 'No. Go, tell others.' So here I am, being his disciple where he wants me to be – telling you – telling you to turn your lives about, asking you to trust him – trust him with everything.

A Prayer

Jesus, thank you for cleansing me, for your healing words and your faith in me. Help me to keep my eyes on you – to remember your words, 'Go, tell the others.' And then enable me to do so. Amen.

In Heaven

I was terrified of coming here – of having to eat my way through a banquet. All those people around the table; a long, narrow table. You breaking the bread and sharing it out, everyone eating and enjoying themselves . . . the noise, the laughter – and the food! Yet, I never did see any of it. The table has never groaned under the weight of bowls and dishes, piled up with food, no one has a full plate in front of them – the table's bare, Lord Jesus, it's bare.

Bare, except for elbows . . . hands resting peacefully . . . hands, palm upwards, perhaps with a piece of bread in them – manna perhaps?

So where's the threat, Lord?

The Reply

Child, there is none. All that food, it's not *all* for you, just some – if you want it. You don't *have* to eat stomach-filling food to be fed – not here. I am with you, I shall fill you.

A Prayer

Lord Jesus, please come to me, fill me to the very brim with yourself, Lord. Let me feel your overwhelming love pour into me. Amen.

Jesus Walks on the Water
Matthew 14:22-27

Our arms were killing us! Let's face it, try as we may, we were getting nowhere – nowhere at all. Somehow, it didn't seem right without him. The boat seemed empty – something missing.

We'd been rowing for hours. I was pulling with all my might at the oars, straining against the weight of the sea, but the stormy waves carried us back to where we'd just rowed from.

I tilted my head back, gritted my teeth to take the next strain of the oar and then – then I saw Jesus coming towards us . . . walking between the waves. Not one wave broke over him . . . there was chaos all around . . . but not on him. There we were, being tossed about – but not Jesus. Oh no, he just sort of made his way towards us, weaving in and out amongst the spume. The waves . . . well, they sort of missed him – passed him by – they made a kind of path for him. Or was it that Jesus made his own path to us? And then his voice, so calm – calm in *that* storm! 'Take heart, it is I.'

Now, of course, I realise just what he did for us – but for my part, I see that I was in a mess, getting nowhere, in too deep. I was in my own storm which was overwhelming me. I wasn't coping.

Suddenly, there was Jesus. Jesus, walking over the troubled waters to reach me; Jesus, calming my fears – and the seas; it is Jesus who walks through the chaos of my life, my own storms and shows his love for me.

A Prayer

Lord Jesus, *you are*. You are everything and truly the Son of God. Without you I am helpless. You calm the waters of my fears, you dry the waters of my tears. You take the flotsam of my shipwreck and make me into a new vessel. Lord Jesus, thank you. Amen.

Mary Magdalene at the Open Tomb
John 20:11-18

I had to see him, just one more time. I *needed* to see him – he was my everything, my all . . . and he was dead. Oh, his poor, poor body, wounded and torn – cut – those awful holes where the nails had been driven through. We'd covered him so carefully, with such love and tenderness . . . I *had* to see him . . . just once more.

So there I stood – at the mouth of the tomb – expecting to find him, still wrapped and oh, so dear to me; but . . . nothing . . . empty; just this emptiness. As empty as I had been over the past few days. The tomb, my Lord's tomb – empty. I couldn't believe it. Such deep, immense, immeasurable pain I had . . . my Lord – gone! In my sobbing state of bewilderment, I turned away. The gardener asked me for whom I searched; whom else would I be searching for? Who else lay in this tomb? He seemed a kindly man – someone I could trust, that gardener, so I asked him where they'd taken his body.

It was when he said my name, 'Mary', that I knew. It was my Lord's voice – his own dear, soft voice. Through tear-blurred eyes I looked again at this kindly man – could it really be? Could it possibly be my Jesus? Could his confusing promise to return be real? Was it *now*? Here, in front of me? Had I not recognised the one I loved most? He didn't *look* the same, yet he *was* the same.

TOUCHING THE HEM

Oh, then the joy, the laughter through the tears, how my heart sang! How I longed to dance with him . . . to hold him . . . to touch his hand . . . his face. How fast I ran! Eager to tell you all the good news. My Lord Jesus *is* alive – alive and well, alive and whole . . . *alive*.

A Prayer

Lord Jesus, you came to me in my distress and though I had not recognised *you,* you knew *me.* I searched for you – you found me. Jesus, you are alive. Keep me alert when I am with others, may their words be your words, their hug be your hug. Dear Lord, don't let me miss *you* in the people I meet today. Amen.

My Cross

I lost my cross today, Lord. Yesterday I was wearing it, and today it was gone. I thought I'd find it, but as the day wore on, my searching became more frantic. I started to pick up papers and then put them down again – I kept going over the same ground, looking, searching – in silly places – but it couldn't be found. I began to panic. My cross, which I'd had for so many years, it was a part of me, my cross.

I found my cross today, Lord. It was lying in an unexpected place – yet right on top, ready for me to see it – if only I'd looked! I'm wearing it again now.

Lord Jesus, I realised, in my searching for the cross, how important it was in my life – your cross, Lord . . . *you*. Thank you for my lesson, and for showing me another reason for wearing it with so much love. I've found *you* again, Jesus: you were there all the time, just waiting to be found.

Jesus' Reply

Child, I'm always with you – you just put me down for a while. In your business, I was pushed aside. It's all right; I know it was unintentional and I stayed with you anyway. Thank you for picking me up again – I'm pleased to be back.

A Prayer

Thank you, Lord, for reminding me that I don't need to search in obscure places to find you. You are everywhere. Thank you for forgiving me, for understanding. Lord, please teach me to be more attentive. I was lost without you. Amen.

Zacchaeus
Luke 19:1-10

I did so want to see this man Jesus. I did so want to be a part of the crowd. I *knew* I wouldn't be able to see – so it was the tree for me. But it was more than that. I was hiding.

The truth is . . . I was afraid. Afraid of all the wrong things I'd done.

Afraid of the people crowding round. Me – a tax collector – made rich by my greed. Made grand by stealing from *them*. I see that now!

It was when he stopped – stopped right under the tree. He *knew* I was there and he called to me: 'Zacchaeus, hurry down.' How did he know my name? How did he know I was there? His face was alight with laughter and joy as he looked up at me – as if he'd found something precious. I felt I was the only one who mattered – in all that great crowd of people. He'd sought – and chosen – *me!*

The crowd closed in, but I didn't feel threatened any more . . . it's strange . . . standing there, in front of Jesus, nothing seemed to matter – except him. Suddenly, I wanted to give everything to him. I wanted to be whole and free from my bad ways. I wanted to give back what I had taken. I could see how badly I'd treated others – how greedy I had been – and I wondered . . . had I really climbed a tree in order to see that? Had my height . . . the blight of my life . . . turned out to be my saving grace?

A Prayer

Lord Jesus, thank you for searching for me and for your saving love. Please let me see that no matter where I hide, or where I am, you love me and you will find me and bring me home. Lord Jesus, thank you for choosing me. Amen.

Jesus Turns Water into Wine
John 2:1-11

I wouldn't have *dreamed* of touching those vessels, not for anyone – but we all knew Mary. She was always so polite to us . . . she treated us with respect. Mary smiled at us and as she passed us, she quietly asked us to do anything Jesus asked. We *couldn't* refuse – he was her son, and you could see she loved him.

Those vessels were empty. Empty and bone dry . . . waiting to be used for the purification process. Jesus asked us to fill them with water . . . it took us a while, but we filled them to the brim. And all the while, Jesus stood by us – watching, with concern in his eyes and an encouraging smile for us. I smiled back – there's no rule about servants not smiling at guests.

As the last jar was filled, I turned to Jesus – pleased with the completion of the task . . . glad that I had been able to serve this man with the patient smile and kindly face. I wasn't expecting him to ask me to draw out the water from the freshly filled jars. I wanted to question him, there seemed to be no sense in his request – until I obeyed. The water . . . was wine!

Startled, I spun round to Jesus, my questioning eyes meeting his; he just looked at me, as if nothing untoward had happened, and told me to take some to the Chief Steward. Hiding all emotion, I did what was requested – all the time, wondering how it had happened. How could water turn into wine? Baffled, I walked back to my place and then, as realisation crept into my thoughts, I stopped. Jesus stood just a little way from me. His eyes were alight with happiness as I watched him talking to his friends, but he looked at me, standing stock still . . . stunned . . . for I realised that I had just witnessed a miracle.

Everything I had heard about Jesus must, then, be true – that he was the Son of God. And as I stood there, trying to come to terms with my thoughts, I realised that I had been staring at Jesus – and that he had been watching me, with a look of warmth and understanding, waiting for me to come to my own decision – my own conclusions.

In surprise and delight, I smiled at him, sorry for having stared – but Jesus simply raised his hand to me, in friendship and acknowledgement of my silent request to follow and to serve him.

I often recall that day, for it was while I was filling the jars that I accepted the emptiness in my own life. I remember the look in Jesus' face as he spoke to Mary: 'Woman, my time has not yet come.' Yet he obeyed her request with love and grace . . . despite the touch of fear which was in his eyes. And I recall with deep gratitude and humility how Jesus welcomed my request to follow him. It isn't easy, being a servant of the Lord, but I am so . . . happy.

A Prayer

Lord Jesus, thank you for accepting me as I am,
for standing by me as I come to my decisions.
Help me to see the job through, so that I may hear you say, 'Well done, my good and faithful servant.' Amen.

Bartimaeus, the Blind Man
Mark 10:46-52

It must have taken courage – to shout out to someone you couldn't see, to shout and go on shouting when others were telling you to stop. It must have taken courage to *go* to someone you couldn't see, to walk blindly and go on walking, with people crowding all around. I wonder how it felt – to leave the cloak of security behind? I wonder if *I'd* have been brave enough to step out blindly with trust and faith as my only guides to Jesus . . .

I was desperate! I was so afraid he wouldn't hear me – so scared he'd walk on by. I didn't need the noise of the crowd to tell me he was approaching – the ground had been vibrating for ages with the approach of many people. I knew he was *close* – but *where* was he? With arms outstretched, I called and cried, 'Jesus, Son of David, please – oh please – hear me! In my unclean, disabled state, help me!'

I thought he hadn't heard; then, for a moment, it went quiet . . . in the stillness, I heard someone speaking . . . a soft voice, gently questioning. I couldn't catch the words, just the stillness of so many breaths being held. Suddenly, I felt a tap on the shoulder – how I jumped! 'Get up, man, take heart – Jesus is waiting for you. He wants you to go to him.'

I am the luckiest man alive, for the first thing I saw – was Jesus. Jesus' loving eyes; his smiling face. He shared in my laughter, wiped away my tears, was moved by my overwhelming joy. When he started walking, I walked too – with him. I joined the throng of people and followed him, joyous and whole. I don't know what happened to my cloak . . . I never looked back!

A Prayer

Lord Jesus, thank you for being close enough for me to reach you. Give me the faith to know that you will hear me when I call – and the courage to go on calling for you when you seem so far away. Amen.

Suffer Little Children to Come unto Me

To the Lord

Lord, you don't really mean to call her to your side, do you? She's too young – just a child. Lord, after all that surgery, the consultant can't eradicate the disease. It's you or no one now – her life is in your hands. Please, can't you help her? Don't you see her pale face – the grey lines like half-moons under her eyes? Lord, can't you hear her when she cries . . . can't you hear me? Dear Jesus, where are you?

The Reply

My child, I am holding you in your anguish, I am catching the tears that fall. Trust me, my child, I am with you.

To the Lord

Another operation, Lord, another term off school – yet we still have her here with us . . . help me with my faith, I do love you. God, my Father, I know she's yours and that you love her – but, she's mine, too, Lord . . . she's mine too!

The Reply

Child, I know. I see your hurt and your fear . . . see, I have sent a messenger to you . . . someone you know and love. Listen to him and obey.

To the Lord

Another operation, Lord, but performed by a different surgeon – the one suggested by your messenger. Thank you for his skill and for his willingness to spend hours rebuilding what the disease has taken away.

Twelve Years Later . . .

Just look at this little miracle, Lord. A perfect replica of her mum. Tiny hands and feet – a strong pair of lungs, all 6lb of her, held so proudly in her daddy's arms.

A Prayer

God, my Father, thank you. Thank you for your miracle in saving my child's life – and for letting her have the miracle of giving life to her own child. Lord, it was hard to hold on to my faith – but you love me and have faith in me always – please keep me worthy of such love and trust. Amen.

The Woman at the Well
John 4:3-42

He was just sitting there . . . propped up against the well . . . to be honest, he looked all in – shattered, exhausted. I suppose that's why I felt it was safe to approach the well and draw water – even though he *was* a Jew and I a Samaritan. I nearly dropped the bucket when he spoke to me . . . I wasn't expecting it!

All he wanted was a drink: at least, that's what he *said* he wanted – I have an idea he'd been waiting for me – then we got chatting. I began to relax . . . I wanted to sit down beside him . . . rest my weary back against the well, too. He gave me a sense of worth – made me feel important – I felt . . . safe. When he mentioned my 'husband', I knew I couldn't lie to him . . . yet . . . we'd only just met!

He *knew*. He knew I had no husband – he knew everything about me – yet, still, he talked to me . . . gave me a place in his heart . . . offered me this spring of living water – I didn't understand, at the time!

There was something about this man. It must have shown on my face, because when I told the other villagers, they believed me! They followed me back to the well . . . he treated us with love and respect. We didn't want him to leave us, but he had other people to teach – other people to reach. When he left, we were changed . . . *I* was changed.

TOUCHING THE HEM

It was just an ordinary day – strange how you never know who's around the corner!

I just want to serve Jesus now, and as I draw water from this same old well, I cast my eyes down to the place where he sat, and remember where and how my new life began . . . and I'm always so thankful.

A Prayer

Lord Jesus, thank you for waiting for me, for coming into my ordinary days and turning them into something special. Help me to remember that you're with me every day – always, even when I seem to have lost you – and that I, too, have had my unexpected moments of surprise with you. Amen.

Trust

Look at those two boys on the bike, Lord! One sitting on the saddle, the other standing with all his weight on the pedals and leaning on the handlebars, guiding the bike. They are both far too big for it, yet they *are* propelling forward. Lord, what makes those two lads think that the one tiny spindle which holds the pedal in place will hold? If the spindle snaps, they'll both fall off. It is invisible to their eyes yet all their trust is in it. Thank you for my lesson, Lord. All my trust is in you – I will not fall – for you bear my weight. You are my balance, my brakes and my invisible spindle. You are my whole support. My life is in you, Lord, you will not let me fall.

The Reply

Hooray! At last, child, you have my message.
For a brief moment, you *know* my love for you
and my guiding power. Come, child, let us
celebrate – for tomorrow you will struggle again.

A Prayer

At last, Lord, I have your message. Help me to
remember this moment so that when I struggle
tomorrow, I will smile as I recall our celebration
of laughter together. Thank you for the traffic jam
that made your message possible. Amen.

Jesus Heals a Paralytic
Mark 2:2-5

They carried me so carefully, my four friends. They must have been tired, but they didn't show it . . . it wasn't an easy journey . . . lots of bumpy ground to get over.

We were so excited – full of joy and hope – until we saw the crowd of people standing outside the door. My friends clambered up on to the roof. Left alone on my mat, unable to join in their quest to reach Jesus, I felt so . . . *helpless*.

When they lifted me up, I saw a gap in the roof – a hole made especially for me, a chance for me to reach Jesus.

It was scary, being let down through the roof. As I was being lowered, a sudden hush settled in the room. I caught glimpses of disbelieving eyes . . . angry eyes . . . disdaining eyes. Then I caught sight of loving eyes . . . forgiving eyes . . . *his* eyes. I just kept looking. He seemed too important for me to lose sight of . . .

I wonder if he saw the love and absolute faith I had for him in my face – for in those few moments of our eyes meeting, I'm *sure* Jesus healed me.

It was the gentleness in his voice that made me get up . . . his smile . . . the assurance in his eyes . . . somehow, I *knew* I could do it. My knees didn't even buckle – I was as strong as anyone else in that room. I cried – I couldn't help it.

You know, when I walked out and greeted my friends, they were different. And I remembered that, as I looked back up to the roof, I saw their faces peering in . . . and I'm positive Jesus saw them as well. So when Jesus told me that *my* sins were forgiven, I'm *sure* that Jesus forgave them as well. I'm sure because, well, now they want to follow Jesus too. Later, I went back – to mend the hole in the roof.

A Prayer

Lord Jesus, thank you for your healing love and for friends who carry me over the rough ground. Dear Lord, help me to mend any damage I may have done to others and may they see *you* through me. Amen.

A King's Journey
Matthew 2:1-2

It was seeing the star that started this journey. I'd never seen anything like it before. So large – so *bright* – and such a strange shape.

The star's brightness beckoned me to follow its guiding light . . . to seek and find . . . *that's* what I felt within me. I had no choice but to follow.

Some thought me an eccentric – more money than sense, thinking I could find the source of that star. But then I met others who had seen it – and they, too, were following its light. We journeyed together, sharing the wonder . . . wondering what we would find at the end of our search – wondering if we *would* find the baby . . .

So here I am, in Bethlehem . . . I, a king – kneeling before *my* king. I, in all my splendour, kneeling on this grubby, dirty, stable floor – and not caring. I, known throughout my lands, hoping that this tiny babe will know – and love – me. I, the supposed eccentric, kneeling with head bowed . . . humbled and in awe. I, a stranger, kneeling at Jesus' manger.

A Prayer

Lord Jesus, I don't want to be a stranger to you. Please stay in my life, and let your guiding light be bright enough for me to follow. Lord, help me to be a light to others – that they may find you also. Amen.

Doors
Luke 13:22-28

You stand at the door of my heart and knock, Lord, and I joyously open wide the door and pray that you will enter. Then I look inside and see what you will see. I long to say, 'Come in, excuse the mess!' Lord – *could* you?

And as I survey this mess, I wonder . . . when the time comes for me to knock on *your* door . . . will I be able to enter into your Kingdom? Will you recognise me amongst the rubble that is within me? Lord, please don't turn me away.

> *The Reply*
>
> Child, how could I *not* come in? Did you not invite me to enter? It doesn't matter about the mess in your heart, I am here already – to heal you and to help you. Child, I know you *now*! I will recognise you wherever you are – did I not say that I would go on before you, to prepare a place for you? When you come knocking on my door, I'll be the one to open it! I will want to pull you in with my joyous welcome.
>
> Child, you love me; you heard me and responded to my call and *that's* all I ask for. Come, throw away these fears and fill your heart with joy. I love you, and I will never leave you.

A Prayer

Lord Jesus, thank you for loving me. Help me to sweep clean the discarded dreams, hopes and hurts that litter the spaces within me and fill them, Lord, with your presence, your spirit, your peace. Amen.

God's Promise

Child, see how the waves rush to the shore . . . see how they flow, sometimes gently lapping, sometimes large and crashing. That's how I long to come to you, child. See how my waves change direction in order to fill every part of you . . . and as you are drawn to the movement of the waves, you will hear their sound and recognise my voice calling to you.

Lord Jesus, you came to me in my fears and promised that I should find you in the quiet moments – and you have kept your promise, Lord, for here I stand, in the stillness of the warm, dark night, watching the waves as they rush over huge, smooth rocks. And as I stand here, watching their constant motion, I hear your voice penetrate deep into my heart. With happy surprise and greatly humbled, I respond – come, free me from fear, so that I may be filled with your love.

> *A Prayer*
>
> **Lord God, thank you for keeping your promises to me – help me to keep mine to you. Remind me often, Lord, of this moment, so that I may not forget your ever-loving presence as you lead me onwards. Amen.**

The Man Born Blind
John 9:1-7

I wasn't doing anything; just sitting, waiting, listening. That's all. I heard voices discussing me – men blaming my blindness on sin. But another voice – a soft, gentle, quiet voice – told them they were wrong, that I'd been *born* blind . . . how did he know? I swear, I'd never met him before – I'd have recognised his voice, I'm good at voices . . . and I'm good at sounds.

That's how I knew he was approaching me: his step was *so* light. Yet . . . I could sense there was something special about him – perhaps that's why I wasn't afraid when he stooped down towards me.

I felt his love . . . his care . . . his breath on my face, as he said I was made for God's purpose. I, a blind man . . . needed by God!

I heard a quiet, spitting sound . . . then I felt gentle fingers touch my eyelids – and something being spread on to them. Something sticky, cloying, gritty . . . mud! And, all the time, I felt the soft breath of this man on my face . . . he breathed peace into me. I wasn't afraid.

The gritty earth set hard over my eyes. It felt . . . *heavy*. The man stepped away – I felt his withdrawal. I wanted him near me again. He was out of the reach of my senses. I wanted him back.

Then I heard his voice telling me to bathe in the pool nearby. As the mud washed away, I began to see colour . . . shapes . . . I saw water . . . my hands. I turned . . . and there he was . . . that kind, soft-voiced, *gentle* man . . . *Jesus. I saw Jesus.* It was *he* who had healed me.

That pool, it was called the Pool of Siloam, which means 'sent'. Jesus said that I'd been sent by God. When he left, his words ran through my mind . . . he said he was the light of the world and that darkness was coming – I wondered about that. I had been in darkness, now I have light . . .

They killed him – they killed Jesus. But I still have his light burning within me.

Now, whenever I feel a gentle breeze on my face, I look down at the mud . . . and remember.

A Prayer

Lord Jesus, thank you for reminding me that when the mud clears, you will still be here beside me. Send me out, Lord, as your light, and may I burn brightly for you – always. Amen.

Simeon
Luke 2:25-35

They gave the child to me . . . I must have held hundreds of babies . . . but this one *felt* different. The babe came to me willingly and as he settled himself into my arms, something happened within me – as if this child was transferring something of himself to me.

And I realised: here was my moment . . . at last. Here, after years of patient waiting, was God's promise to me; for here, in my arms, I held the child Jesus – the Messiah, the Saviour of the world.

Briefly, I hugged the child closer to me and as I looked up from his tiny face, I caught sight of his mother and a deep stab of anguish coursed through me – for I knew in that moment that she would suffer greatly.

Inwardly I cried, 'Ah no, dear Lord, do not let her heart be pierced.' Mary has delivered your son to me for dedication to you, dear Lord, is that not enough?

As surely as the Spirit sent me to the Temple, so it led me to speak – to tell of the greatness and wonder her child would bring – to warn her that she would know grief, a deep, burning, unbearable grief.

SIMEON

One last look at that special babe, one last stroke of my thumb against his tiny face, and I released him from my loving arms into those of his mother . . . and as the weight of this child shifted away from me, so a deep, deep peace settled into me.

My Lord has kept his promise – I have seen the Messiah. And so I smile . . . with my last sigh of goodbye.

A Prayer

Lord God, my Father, give me the patience to wait for your promises of fulfilment. Keep me faithful to you, Lord, and may I know the comfort of your peace. Amen.

Jairus' Daughter
Mark 5:21-42

My daughter was dying – dying, do you hear? I *had* to find Jesus – I ran all the way and as I ran, I cried, 'Jesus, where are you? – I must find Jesus.' I saw a crowd and knew he must be in it somewhere. My eyes began searching . . . my heart searched too . . . but . . . how would I *know* him? How could I find him?

Jesus . . . found *me*. His eyes . . . his face, as he watched me frantically searching . . . I saw love and understanding in his expression. Such a sense of relief ran through me . . . I *had* recognised him. I knew in that moment – that he'd been waiting for me! I fell to my knees: 'Dear Jesus, please – my daughter is dying. Please . . . come, save my child.' Distraught, I could say no more.

A woman in the crowd stopped his progress – how *could* I be cross with her? She had need of him too. They told me my daughter had died. Too late now, for Jesus . . . I felt his hand on my shoulder – a warm, comforting, *strong* hand – and his voice, soft . . . gentle . . . kind . . . *assured:* 'She's not dead, only sleeping. Come.'

We entered her room – so still, calm, *deadly* quiet. And in the hush, Jesus walked towards her . . . took her hand in his. Surely, in that moment, she was as much his child as she is

TOUCHING THE HEM

mine, for his love for her shone through . . . his very gaze on her small, still body showed his authority over her as he told her to wake up and arise.

He kept hold of her hand . . . his look of tenderness as she opened her eyes . . . it told of his deep, deep love for her – his pure delight at helping her to sit up. He laughed as he watched her reciprocate, smile at him with love.

Then he left us . . . went on his way. But he left us changed. Truly, I have seen a miracle – the miracle of life over death. Every day, I thank God for the gift of my daughter. Every day I travel further along the road, telling people the good news of Jesus. He saved my daughter – but he came to save you, too. Turn around, follow this new path – *his* path – you'll not regret it.

A Prayer

Lord Jesus, I see miracles of life all around – and I take them for granted. Keep me more alert to your presence, so that I may follow your path and reach others with your good news. Amen.

It's All Right

It's all right to love – and to let go. To let go and still love . . . isn't it, Lord?

It's all right to feel the deep pain, sometimes – that deep, deep pain, isn't it?

It's all right to laugh, dance, sing – to remember for a moment . . . and then to go on laughing, dancing and singing . . . isn't it, Lord?

Is it all right to fly free from the past – like a kite soaring – to stretch out my arms and feel the freshness of the day, the newness in me . . . the release of too much need in another?

Is it all right to love – but differently – to keep my distance, yet acknowledge the absence?

It's all right to hope, in the knowledge that *you* know the truth – to go on trusting in *you*, Lord, isn't it?

> *The Reply*
>
> My dear child of the faithful heart – how I do love you. And yes, it is all right.

A Prayer

Lord Jesus, thank you for holding on to me while I learned to let go; for showing me the way forward when I wanted to look back; for giving me your steadfast love – always. Amen.

Malchus, the High Priest's Slave and Soldier
Luke 22:49-50

I say he was innocent. Yes, I *was* ready for a fight, as ready as the rest of you, but *he* wasn't! He just stood there, gently chastising us for carrying our weapons. Something in his voice stopped me in my tracks . . . the silence . . . not one of us made a sound after he spoke – not one.

It was as he healed my ear that something happened . . . Jesus looked deep into my eyes and for one blessed moment, I felt his love for me . . . and then, as my blood trickled through his fingers, I saw a deep anguish . . . I almost felt his pain, his fear . . . then, with great care, he gently cradled the side of my face in his hand and stepped back. I swear he saw my change of heart . . . and he *forgave me*.

For it was at that moment that I realised I could no longer be a soldier – that's why I held back from you all . . . as you led him away . . . I *couldn't* go along with it. I *couldn't*.

I keep seeing the love and forgiveness in his eyes – did you see how black the sky became?

Did you hear the thunder? Did you see the misery of those who stayed with him to the end?

Did *he* see *me* standing in the background – waiting? Wanting to say 'thank you' and 'I'm sorry'? Did he see?

A Prayer

Lord Jesus, you forgave us then, you forgive us now. Thank you for dying for me. Please Lord, I pray, make me a worthy soldier for you. Amen.

Mary, the Mother of Jesus
Luke 1:26-38

She must have been startled, when Gabriel dropped in to visit – when he called her 'holy' and 'blessed' – and then asked her to have God's child. And she, a mere child herself.

It must have taken courage to leave home, to journey – alone – to Elizabeth . . . to wait quietly for Joseph's decision and then to journey with him to Bethlehem. She must have had trust, Lord, trust in you when no place could be found – and she already in labour . . . it must have been *love*, Lord, a special kind of love . . . Mary, the mother of your child.

> And all the time, Lord, you *knew*.
> You watched and helped her see it through.
> You put people along her way,
> and safe places for her to stay.
> You loved her too, Lord – a special kind of love –
> for Mary, the mother of your child.

Now, as I consider Mary, how you stayed with her, carried and protected her, I see that you do the same for me every moment of every day. You're here beside me – sitting, walking, laughing, crying – you, Lord, my constant companion and friend.

TOUCHING THE HEM

You have put people along my way,
given me safe places to stay.
Thank you for my blessings, Lord,
for the children who are also yours –
may they live to fight your cause.
This comes with love, Lord, a special kind
    of love . . .
from me, another mother of your child.

A Prayer

Father God, you know me and have plans for me.
Give me the ears to hear your call, the sense to
recognise your voice, and the courage to obey –
to step out in faith, Lord – as Mary did. Amen.

I Am the Good Shepherd
John 10:11

It feels like you've been leading me up a long, steep climb, Lord, and my path is slippery with loose stones. During this climb, Lord, my foot *has* slipped – often – but I have *never* fallen. As surely as I know I must follow this path, I know you are before me, leading me onwards. I see the brow up ahead – yet I don't know what lies beyond it. Lead on, dear Lord, let me not lose sight of you. After the rough comes the smooth – so I trust you to lead me to green pastures on the other side.

The Reply

Child, keep trusting, keep following, stay true to the path. I know the ground on which you tread – I have you in my sights. The path is steep, but you can do it – see how far you have travelled. Come child, take my hand, I will not let you fall.

A Prayer

God, my Father, thank you for giving me encouragement and for giving me your hand to steady my journey. Lord, when I look back, may I see only beauty; for even shards of glass which cut deep can, from a distance, throw out rays of radiant colours. Keep me with you, Lord, this climb is too steep without you. Amen.

Changes

I don't want to say goodbye – it's too hard, too painful. Lord, can't you change this bit of my life and keep these, my special people, in it? I do love them so.

The Reply

Child, no. You can't stay here, I need you – and them – elsewhere, doing other work for me. Have faith in me, take the hand I am holding out to you – it *is* for you. Come, this is the path I want you to take: in time, you will see that my way is less painful than you imagine – come, child, one step, then another, away from the life you knew, away from the life *you* had planned – and into the life *I* have prepared and planned for you. Come, I am calling you, I have need of you.

A Prayer

Lord Jesus, here I am. As I take hold of your hand, lead on, Lord, let me but follow. All my faith is in you. Amen.

'The Holy Spirit that Has Been Given to Us'
Romans 5:5

I've got the Holy Spirit! You've given it to me, Lord, deep here, in my heart. It's all mine – yet my heart is all yours. Is that how you are in me . . . and I in you? Your love poured into my heart, and then from my heart into yours? An ever-flowing cycle of love between the two of us – ever growing, ever changing, sometimes still, calm, sometimes a rushing wind . . . an awareness so strong, it's almost overwhelming.

> *The Reply*
>
> My precious child, at last! For some time you have known of your love for me . . . known my Spirit was within you. Knowing this has helped you – but you needed the stillness of this peaceful room to allow yourself to acknowledge all you *know* and all you *feel* for me (and I for you) – it's *real* child, it's *real*.
>
> Child, just as the Disciples sat in the upper room waiting and wondering, so have you waited and wondered in your room. Welcome to your Pentecostal moment. Come, now that you know my Spirit is within you, let us step out together – there is much work to be done.

A Prayer

Lord Jesus, thank you for sharing your love with me. Show me the way, that I may show others your love for them – so that they, too, may come to find you in the centre of their lives, as you live in them . . . and they in you. Amen.

The Shepherd's Tale
Luke 2:8-18

I was just a boy when the angels came to tell us about Jesus. In a daze, and incredibly excited, we rushed down the mountain side . . . towards Bethlehem . . . our eyes fixed on the star as it guided us.

At the stable, we stopped. Inside, it was *exactly* as the angel had said. Mary was there, with Joseph . . . and the baby. I crept forward, gazing in amazement at the tiny, sleeping child. Mary smiled at me – as if she understood my wonder at this perfect miracle – then, gently, she lifted him up and offered him to me. Mary let *me* hold the baby.

I held him carefully, tenderly. As he slept on in my arms, the other shepherds explained about the angels and their message of joy and hope – and as they told the grown-ups, I told Jesus. I told him about the angels' singing; I sang the song to him softly and told him how precious he was, how special – and all the time he slept on . . . safe . . . in the cradle of my arms.

I didn't *want* to leave him but we had to get back to our sheep; so I kissed his tiny forehead and knelt to lay him back in his crib. The baby was awake! With joy in my heart, I smiled at him . . . his eyes seemed so alert . . . so . . . focused and as I whispered 'Hello, Jesus – and goodbye', he looked into my eyes and curled his tiny fingers around my thumb. He held on to me, as if I was important, and then we left. We left to continue our lives as shepherds, tending our flocks and gazing into the night sky – remembering.

I'm too old to go up into the mountains now – too old to tend my flock of sheep – but I *am* still a shepherd. I keep watch on all these children in the village and, as they gather round me, I tell them stories and teach them songs – the one they like best is the song of the angels and the story of the lowly little shepherd boy who held the baby Jesus in his arms . . .

They *like* to hear how that boy's life was changed, how Jesus clung to him and how, as he grew up, he noticed that the lines across his thumb knuckle were *exactly* the place where the baby Jesus had gripped his thumb. And then, I show the children – the descendants of those first shepherds – that they, too, have these lines on *their* thumbs as a reminder that Jesus loves them and that he will *always* be with them.

A Prayer

Lord Jesus, you called the fishermen as your disciples and made them fishers of men. You called the shepherds and, in the telling of their story, made them shepherds of people. Take me, dear Lord, gather me to you and teach me – so that I, too, may learn to spread your word. Thank you for my thumb-knuckle lines, Lord – a constant reminder of Father, Son and Holy Spirit, and that you will *never* let me go. Amen.

The Widow's Mite
Luke 21:1-4

I had given *everything* . . . yet to them it wasn't enough. With a sneer of derision, they turned their backs and walked off together and I was left standing alone . . . I could do nothing but square my shoulders as I felt the blow of rejection.

Feeling a deep sadness, I turned away, shame and pain my companions. My offering had cost me much hardship – for I had given my all. And then, Jesus, I saw *you* . . . standing there, watching. No sign of derision in *your* eyes – instead, I saw love . . . compassion . . . *understanding*.

You knew about the pain of rejection, the sting of cruel words . . . the emptiness of solitude. Dear Lord, I never said a word, yet you understood my plight and blessed me where I stood – for as I gave my all to you in my offering of two small coins, you gave me yourself . . . you blessed me with your love, your smile . . . you gave me back my dignity.

As I look back on that day, Jesus, as I see their eyes so full of scorn, I remember *your* look of love for me – and I recall with the same sense of amazement that *you* were there . . . standing among us . . . and *they*, so wrapped up in their own self-importance, had missed you.

A Prayer

Lord Jesus, thank you for your compassion and understanding. Stay near me, Jesus, and let me never forget that you are here – standing, watching, in every situation. Keep reminding me, Lord, that it's quality that matters to you – the *quality* of giving. All I have is yours – help me to use it wisely, that your name may be glorified. Amen.

The Man at the Pool
John 5:2-9

For thirty-eight years I'd been living near the sheep's gate – waiting, near the poolside. Thirty-eight years of disappointed plans – of thinking I'd make it *this* time, of reaching my goal, but someone else always beat me to it.

I realised how weak I had become – and that, although the distance to the pool remained the same, over the years, my goal *seemed* further away . . . less attainable . . . I became weary of propelling myself down the path, alone, of hearing the voices of others calling 'Come, quickly' when the water stirred . . . of reaching the poolside and *never* going in.

But still, I kept trying . . . waiting patiently for the next time . . . I clung to the thought that surely my turn would come – that *somehow*, I would be healed.

I wasn't expecting Jesus to come! He arrived quietly with his friends, looking all around; then he saw me . . . came over to where I lay and smiled down at me . . . I saw love in his face and compassion in his eyes. Speechlessly, I gazed up at him, aware of a deep stirring within me – a sense of excitement, trust and . . . *love* . . . for this stranger.

Jesus asked if I wanted to be well. With tears of desperation in my eyes, I stared at him. I looked from Jesus to the water

– and then back to his face. Hope grew in me . . . did he mean it? Did Jesus *really* mean it? I felt his love wash over me . . . heard his voice speak the words: 'Pick up your mat and walk' . . . and I did. In fact, I did more than that – I danced at the water's edge! I'm dancing still.

My steps are a little slow as I follow him – but, like the good shepherd he is, he stops and waits for me to catch up. My heart skips with my feet when his eyes alight on me with such love – love for a man who had waited for thirty-eight years at the sheep's gate before his true shepherd found him.

A Prayer

Lord Jesus, thank you for finding me and for your cleansing love. Give me the faith to wait, and the trust to get up and walk – when you call me, Lord. Amen.

Simon the Pharisee
Luke 7:36-50

I thought I'd made it – having Jesus at my house for supper. I felt proud and grand . . . important. Then *she* walked in. How she managed to slip past the doorman, I don't know – but in she came – bold as brass, holding on to her pot as if her life depended on it.

I knew her, of course – didn't we all? Though none of us would *dream* of admitting it in public. Anger coursed through me. I tried to catch my servants' eyes to tell them to evict her, but they were all watching her. With disgust, I looked towards her . . . she was kneeling at Jesus' feet, crying. Her tears spilled on to him – she didn't even have a cloth to wipe them away. She was *ruining* my evening – my special, well-thought-out plans – all put to waste because of this sinful woman.

I looked at Jesus, wondering *why* he was allowing her near him. Why, if he knew so much, hadn't he recognised her for what she was? And then he spoke to me – pointed out all the love this lady had given to him – and how she had *bathed* his feet with her tears – and I, who had so much, had failed to offer my honoured guest the cool freshness of water as he entered my home.

Through my own self-importance, I had failed in my hospitality. In trying to get it so right for *myself*, I had failed in what Jesus was looking for above all else – love. I had not given myself – only my wealth.

I have been humbled beyond measure, but the lesson is learned – for I saw myself as Jesus saw me, though his rebuke was kindly said . . . and love shone in his eyes as he explained about forgiveness – and judgement.

Now my life has changed. I welcome my guests with warmth rather than pomp . . . I offer them water for their comfort. Everyone is invited. Now, I love them with my heart – the way Jesus showed *his* love for me.

A Prayer

Lord God, thank you for loving me and for your guidance – for my humbling moments and lessons learned. Dear God, thank you for being gentle with me. Amen.

The Crippled Woman
Luke 13:10-14

It was his voice which drew me nearer. A soft, kindly voice – yet one with authority. As I crept forward, I watched his feet and listened . . . oh, how I wished I could see his face.

Suddenly, he stopped speaking – took a step towards me, and then stopped. In fear, I waited for his retribution; afraid that he would send me away; but when he next spoke, his voice had changed to one of tenderness, and I heard him call me to him. What was it in his voice which beckoned me? What was it that assured me he was safe to approach? It was kindness, gentleness . . . *love*.

I felt him place his hands on my shoulders . . . he told me that my ailment had left me – that I was healed – and I . . . believed him.

I could feel his hands still resting on my shoulders – and as I struggled to force my neck up, I realised my body was becoming upright. My back, doubled for so many years, straightened – and I looked into the dear face of Jesus.

In surprise, I covered my mouth with my hand and, as tears of gratitude softly fell, he caught one with his finger and, as he wiped it away, he smiled at me with such tenderness as if . . . as if I were *important* to him.

I know now that it is only love which matters . . . pure, heart-filled love . . . for that is how Jesus loves *me* and it was his love which healed me.

I tell my story to anyone who will listen, for I *know* that Jesus loved me – just as I was – yet his love changed me. He made me whole, and gave me a new life. If you want, Jesus will give you life too. He will mend you and lead you – all you need is the *desire* to have faith, the faith to believe, and to have love in your heart.

A Prayer

Lord Jesus, you loved me as I was and you love me now – let me feel your hands on my shoulders as you gently guide me into the future. Amen.

Jesus Heals the Deaf Mute
Mark 7:31-35

Have you any idea what it's like to live in a world of silence? To see mouths move and not know the sound of voices? To see a baby's tear and not hear its cry? To watch running water – wash in it, play in it – and not know the music of its movement? Do you know how good one becomes at reading people's faces, of sensing atmosphere? I do . . . I was deaf . . . once.

I lived in my own solitary world, quietly staying in the background, until Jesus came. I watched him arrive with his friends . . . the atmosphere amongst the townspeople was charged with excitement. I saw my friends chatting together. They looked at Jesus, looked at me, and then looked back at Jesus. I wondered what they were saying to each other – I wanted to join in. They seemed to be thinking . . . and then they came over to me. In their excitement, they talked quickly – I couldn't read what they were saying. They took my by the arms and pulled me forward – and I went with them and then . . . stopped. I could see now that they were leading me to Jesus . . . I didn't know if I wanted to meet him . . . didn't know anything about him . . . I didn't understand why they thought him so important.

Jesus was talking to my friends – they were behaving as if they'd known him all their lives – I think I felt . . . envy. I knew they were talking about me; I saw them say the words 'deaf' and 'can't speak very well'.

Then Jesus looked at me and smiled . . . he stepped towards me and put out his arm – as if to direct me, as if to say 'this way', and I went with him . . . out of the sight of those I knew – just he and I, companions on the road, leading to a quiet place; a place away from staring eyes and curious glances.

Gratefully, I looked at him – I knew my life was about to be changed. And . . . yes . . . I *was* afraid – that's why I appreciated the privacy – and Jesus understood. He just waited patiently, as if he knew my inner turmoil, and then, as I smiled my acceptance of change, he gave me his smile of understanding and gently placed his fingers in my ears. At that moment, my inner voice of doubt disappeared and, instead, trust entered my heart. I watched Jesus as he looked upwards and I saw his mouth move. He touched my tongue – just here – and as he did so, he spoke . . .

I *heard* Jesus speaking. In amazement and wonder I looked at him; I listened as he spoke words of encouragement in a soft, gentle voice . . . I heard a rumble of sound – and as I watched Jesus' loving face crease into a smile, I heard a similar noise from *him* . . . laughter . . . we were laughing together. What a noise we made – what a strange sound laughter is – and how small the words . . . 'thank you'.

It took a while to get used to the change in my life, but I am truly content. I laugh often – for whenever I laugh, I hear the echo of Jesus' laughter, and I wonder if he remembers me and if he knows what a chatter-box I have become . . . for him.

A Prayer

Lord Jesus, thank you for your patience as I learn to change, and for the echoes of laughter. Hold out your arm to me, Lord, and give me the courage to follow you. Amen.

Barabbas
Mark 15:6-15

They swapped him for me . . . how *could* they do that? I, a robber and murderer . . . but I didn't care – then! With a great roar, I shouted, 'Yes!' I couldn't wait to get out there – to wreak havoc once again, to get my revenge on those who had put me away – oh yes, I was ready, all right.

On my way out to freedom, I passed Jesus. He looked *awful* – surely the soldiers hadn't needed to flog him *that* much, had they? The man was more dead than alive . . . I felt sorry for him.

As I drew level with him, he raised his head and looked straight at me . . . I saw the look of acceptance in his weary face . . . and in his eyes, I saw sadness and a deep understanding. I had never felt the sense of guilt before, but I knew it then . . . guilt and humility.

I looked down, unable to hold his gaze . . . I couldn't bear to see such suffering in his eyes . . . and then I walked away – and smiled at a crowd gone mad.

I didn't stay to watch the events of that day, instead, I went home – and wept. I wept for my freedom, which had cost Jesus his life, and, as I wept, the sight of his face came freshly to mind – I again saw the look in his eyes and I began to doubt my plans of revenge . . .

For as long as Jesus hung on that cross, I battled with myself – revenge or forgiveness? Suddenly, I seemed to hear a different voice – a quiet, weary voice – whispering, 'Father, forgive them', and I *knew* it to be the voice of Jesus.

Father, forgive . . . and he – innocent.

At that moment, my inner battle ended and I chose forgiveness.

I could have gone back to my old ways of living, but I decided not to. My friends couldn't understand at first – they told me I was mad, doing an honest day's work – but some of them work with me now. And every now and then, the face of Jesus comes into my mind . . . his eyes meet mine . . . and I know that no matter how difficult my new life becomes, I won't go back on my decision – for I owe it to Jesus . . . the man who exchanged his life – for mine.

A Prayer

Lord Jesus, you died for me – help me to live for you. Amen.

The Ten Lepers
Luke 17:11-19

I thought I had it all – money, friends, *terrific* lifestyle . . . then I got the disease and I lost everything . . . everything.

Hassled out of town, I joined a small colony . . . there were only ten of us. They welcomed me . . . gave me food and shelter. They accepted me as I was. As time passed, I learned how to give . . . how to share . . . I learned a whole new set of values . . . of respect, and how to trust people.

Yet, we had nothing – just ourselves. We heard that a man called Jesus had come into town . . . that he had healed people, had said and done amazing things – and that he was now leaving. So, we shuffled to the edge of the road and waited for him to pass.

We saw Jesus coming, he was with friends and I noticed that *they* had nothing either . . . just each other; they were laughing together – enjoying each other's company. In desperation, we called out to him – he turned and approached us. He must have seen the pleading in our eyes, the trust . . . the *hope* . . . for as Jesus came closer, his eyes registered compassion and then, in a most kind and gentle voice, he simply told us to show ourselves to the high priest. In amazement, we turned as one and, without a second glance, we headed straight to town.

As we walked, I wondered what I would find . . . were my old friends still there . . . would they welcome me back? And then, the thought struck me . . . did *I* want *them*? I stopped walking with the realisation of how much I had changed – how my values had shifted – and as I looked down, deep in thought, I noticed my toes . . . they had flesh on them – new, undamaged flesh. I stood, transfixed in wonder at the healing which had taken place, and I suddenly realised – I had not thanked Jesus.

How I wanted to go on with my friends – to show myself to the priest – but the pull to return to Jesus was stronger. I turned around and called after him and he waited for me to catch up – waited with a welcoming smile – and watched as I struggled to reach him. He laughed with me – as I laughed and cried and praised God on my knees.

I'm sorry the others didn't return with me, for he asked after them; he seemed perplexed, hurt. With a sigh, Jesus looked down at me and then he stretched out his hand towards me and set me on my feet again. The tears of gratitude were wet on my cheeks as Jesus looked at me – really looked – as if he could see deep into my soul. Then he nodded to himself and, with a look of kindness and understanding, he told me to go – that I was well. With a deep sense of regret, I turned around once more and left Jesus.

I never did return to the town, for I no longer needed the security of belongings – they only served to weigh me down. I realised how much I had learned of life during my years of isolation – especially the importance of caring for one another. Now all I carry is the picture, in my mind's eye, of the look of love Jesus gave me as we waved goodbye to each other – and it is *that* love which I share as I tell my story to other travellers who journey along the road with me.

A Prayer

**Lord Jesus, thank you for your healing touch
and for placing some of your travellers in my path
as I walk this new road. Amen.**

The Field of Corn
Luke 6:1-5

The field was bathed in the warm rays of the sun. The corn, beautiful and golden, was ripe for the picking.

We were all so happy and carefree – enjoying the quiet as we peeled away the chaff before eating the grain.

I looked at my group of friends and thought how lucky I was. I looked at Jesus, laughing at some joke, a peaceful expression on his face . . . love in his eyes . . . and I wondered . . . *how* did he ever come to choose *me*? *How* did he come to *love* me – and I him – this much?

We strolled through the field, choosing our ears of corn carefully, sometimes coming together, sharing our harvest with each other, before moving on again.

I turned to Jesus, happily holding out my offering of corn, and, for a brief moment, I caught a glimpse of a message in his eyes . . . it flickered for a moment and then he shut it away and smiled his acceptance of the corn I held out to him.

The moment passed and laughter returned.

Laughter . . . happiness . . . freedom – a perfect day with Jesus.

As I look back on that day, as I recall the look in his eyes, I realise what Jesus was trying to say to me: that the harvest must be ripe . . . and, I see now, how like the field of corn *we* are . . . for are *we* not his harvest? Had Jesus not chosen us as his disciples? We grew with each other . . . shared the same teaching . . . the same bread and wine. We, too, were felled . . . and scattered. We, too, have sown seeds. Jesus' words are our seeds and we are harvesting for Jesus – in readiness for another such perfect day, when he will again look at me with love and accept all that I am as I hold out my palm full of offering once more.

A Prayer

Dear Jesus, thank you for making my small harvest perfect for you – for as you held out your arms on the cross for me, so you blew away the chaff of my imperfect offering. Amen.

Simon
Luke 5:1-11

He didn't seem to notice that I was actually quite tired – and busy. I'd been up all night, had caught nothing, and cleaning my nets had never been my favourite job.

A huge crowd had gathered to hear this teacher called Jesus – but I hadn't expected him to jump into my boat – and I *certainly* was not prepared to push the boat out from dry land again.

About to refuse, I looked at Jesus. He looked tired – yet there was a glint of fun in his eyes as he waited for me to join him.

Leaving the nets unfinished, I walked down to my boat and pushed her out once more. For a while, I sat – with resentment as my companion – and waited for Jesus to finish addressing the crowds from the water. His words reached them perfectly . . . and everyone could see him.

Jesus talked of change – said there was a better way to live . . . I began to listen – *really* listen . . . and I began to think deeply about my own life. I wondered if *I* would ever rise to the challenge of change . . .

When Jesus had finished speaking, he sat down. In silence, I looked at him – his message had touched me. I needed time to let it all sink in – then Jesus broke the silence. He asked me to go into deeper water and to cast out my nets for a catch. I lifted my head to him in amazement. I tried to explain that there *were* no fish – I knew, I had waited all night for a catch! Jesus looked at me, and in his eyes I saw understanding . . . so, I turned the boat around and half-jokingly replied: 'For you, master, anything!'

It was our biggest catch ever – it almost sank the boat. Stunned, I stared at Jesus – he smiled and let out a small chuckle and watched quietly as I struggled with my thoughts. I felt afraid, and humbled beyond words. Looking at Jesus, I fell to my knees. 'Leave me, Jesus, go away . . . I am a sinner.'

I wasn't expecting his answer . . . wasn't expecting his calm acceptance of me, his smile of reassurance, or his voice, gently saying: 'Don't be afraid, come, join me . . . and be a fisher of men.'

As we reached the shore, Jesus stepped out of my boat and held out his hand to me. I took it – and I followed him.

Come, take my hand . . . and I will show you the way to Jesus.

A Prayer

Lord Jesus, I'm scared of change. Hold out your hand to me and lead me onwards – that I may go deeper and cast out my nets for you, Lord. Amen.

Zebedee
Mark 1:19-20

I loved my sons – we got on well together. We used to sit by the lake, peacefully listening to the waves as they rushed over one another in their efforts to reach the shore. Sometimes, we'd sit in the boat, feeling the gentle lapping of water against her sides as we quietly mended our nets.

It was on just such a day that Jesus came. He saw us, peacefully working together. All he said was: 'Follow me', and my boys got up and did just that.

I cried out to them: 'But what about *me* – the boat, the business? What about your *mother*?' A brief hug ... and they were gone ... walking away without a backward glance. In despair, I watched their retreating backs – was that *all*? After a lifetime of loving, could they really leave everything they knew *that* easily?

Numb with pain and shock, I lost all sense of time – then, as I recalled the scene yet again, I suddenly remembered how, as my boys were scrambling to their feet, Jesus had looked at me. We had exchanged glances ... and I remembered the hurt and confusion as I thought: Why are you taking *my* boys? They are my life ... I need them, I can't carry on without them. My eyes had pleaded with his – and Jesus had responded. He had seen my pain and incomprehension – and, just as he was reading the message in my eyes, so I read the message in his. He had need of them also – and his need was greater. Jesus had looked at my two boys with such love . . . friendship . . . and my boys had joined him with such willingness and excitement. Jesus shared a joke with them for I heard their laughter as they walked away.

I hear laughter often when they come home with their friends, freely giving the news as they share in the telling of their adventures. And as I listen to the happy banter between them, I smile to myself – to think I thought I'd never survive without them – and I acknowledge the fact that I needed the oh-so-hard lesson . . . of learning to let go.

Sometimes, as I look at Jesus across the kitchen table, we share a smile. Jesus chose my sons – for his special purpose – and I am so thankful that he has them still.

Now, as I listen to the waves break over each other, I silently bless them both and hope that Jesus will always have need of them – and they of him.

A Prayer

Lord Jesus, sometimes you seem to ask for the impossible. Keep my faith strong as I learn to let go – for I know that you are teaching me in order that I can fulfil your need of me. Amen.

The Raising of the Widow's Son
Luke 7:11-15

Once, I had status – had my own servants – but then I found myself alone . . . totally . . . dreadfully alone . . . and all I could do was cry for my only son who had died. My grief was overwhelming as they carried him out. First my husband, now him – the son whom I had loved so much. I would have given anything to have him returned to me.

I saw a crowd of people approaching and noticed that Jesus was among them – he seemed upset at my distress. He walked towards me . . . talked to me with gentleness and kindness. He placed his hand softly on my arm, and told me to stop crying. Through tear-filled eyes, I looked up, straight into his eyes, so loving and understanding. His look gave me comfort – a sense of peace.

Stunned, I watched as he approached my dead son's coffin. Laying his hand gently on it, he said, 'Young man, get up.' I am sure that not a soul breathed, for the silence was deafening. We watched, transfixed, as my son slowly sat up and rubbed his eyes.

Jesus held my son and guided him back to me. Rooted to the spot, I watched them both as they approached – two such dear people – the one, dazed, and the other so full of love as he handed his companion back to me – my own son, returned from the dead.

I hugged them both! Crying tears of joy, I first held my son, then Jesus. As he slowly released himself from my grasp, Jesus took my hand and placed it over that of my son . . . we were together again, joined by Jesus.

I saw a look of wonder and love for Jesus on my son's face, and I knew that he would want to follow him . . . that he *belonged* to him. I looked at Jesus . . . I looked at the crowd . . . saw their happy faces, heard them praising God for another miracle – and I realised with a start that Jesus had shown me the true meaning of life – and love – and that I, too, belonged to him.

I no longer wanted my own servants. *I* wanted to serve. I no longer needed to be tied down by my possessions – I wanted to give . . . freely.

We sold our home, my son and I, and we gave away everything we owned. We had no need of possessions any more. We are happy. And so, I continue on life's journey with love in my heart for my son . . . and for Jesus, his Saviour – and mine.

A Prayer

Lord God, you heal us sometimes in unexpected ways – thank you. Make of me your faithful follower, Father, for that is all I ask of you – and you of me. Amen.

The River of Life

Look at this river, Lord, as it runs full speed through the garden, its path guided by stones placed on either side of the water – yet it flows freely, rushing and running to meet its destiny.

Amidst all the hurrying, I see small pools of calm – and in those pools lies the debris of twigs and stones which the water could no longer carry. I watch as a small trickle spills over the edge of a rock and joins the main stream again.

The water is laughing and gurgling, dancing and sparkling as it speeds on to its journey's end. And as the river approaches the sea, it disappears underground and the stones come to an end – no channel is needed now, for the water has found its own way to the open, welcoming sea.

As I consider this river, Lord, I see that I am describing my own life's journey. The fast running through each day, the rush and hurry – and the calm times, Lord, when I come to you with my burdens and lay them down at your feet; or when I sit quietly . . . simply being with you . . . before I, too, rejoin my own main stream of life. And, Lord, when I come to my own tunnel at my journey's end, I wonder . . . will I find *you* there, waiting to welcome me?

The Reply

My child, I love you and I am with you always. Come, let us watch this river together. See how I steer a safe passage through the boulders of your journey – how safe are those places of rest and calm. See how I long to take away your burdens – to leave you free to laugh and sing again. Child, when eventually you reach the tunnel of your life, I will be with you . . . leading you into the wide, wide sea . . . of home.

A Prayer

God, my Father, sometimes I feel battered and bruised from the passage through the boulders of life. Hold me gently in the calm of your arms, so that I may return to the bubble of life, and show your way to others, as we follow the flow of the river of life together. Amen.

I Am the Vine, You Are the Branches
John 15:5-6

Lord, I need to be guided, tended, nurtured. Lord, don't leave me as a damaged branch, trailing along the ground – pick me up, wash me clean and put me back in place, so that I can bear fruit for you.

The Reply

Child, I am tending you, you *are* growing. I see tiny buds of new life in you – fresh, and waiting to flourish. Give it time, and have faith during this season of preparation. You are bruised from the pruning, but I am healing you. See, I have wrapped you round a trellis . . .

Soon, child, as the buds of new life develop, you will move on to a different part of the trellis and you will bear fruit. Child, you are one of my branches, and I love you.

A Prayer

God, my Father, thank you for your tender care of me and for your healing love. Help me to be the true branch you wish me to be, and may I be strong enough to support others as I grow. I ask this in Jesus' name. Amen.

The Baptism of Jesus
Matthew 3:13-17

I had only come out to see what the noise was about – I wondered why such a crowd had gathered. Disgruntled with the disruption of my usual solitary routine, I opened the door to send them packing. A group of people told me excitedly that they had followed Jesus here, and that he was at the River Jordan.

Jesus . . . ? Who, on earth, was Jesus?

Curiosity got the better of me! I strolled down to the river's edge, and stood where most of the crowd had gathered. Someone pointed him out to me, but it wasn't necessary, for I had seen for myself a young man, with an air of authority about him – and yet, as he glanced my way, he seemed pleased to see me . . . pleased that I was with the rest of the crowd that was following him. There was something in their eyes . . . something which told me that, although they had nothing, they had found something special. With a jolt of surprise, I knew that, above all, I wanted whatever it was that they had found.

I found myself in the water, longing to be baptised with the others, all of us sharing the same need – wanting a fresh start in life, wanting to be made clean.

THE BAPTISM OF JESUS

My eyes were fixed on Jesus – I saw him wade deep into the water with John, the One Who Baptises, and I watched, spellbound, as they stood together . . . and then blessed and baptised each other.

And, all the while, amongst *us* – the onlookers – there was a stillness; a complete, unbreakable quiet.

Something strange happened on that day, for we all saw a dove appear – as if from nowhere. It seemed to hover over Jesus as he emerged from the water and, just as the dove appeared, so a voice boomed out like thunder across the sky: 'This is my son, whom I love.'

The voice *was* that of God. I know it absolutely . . . and I know that God referred to Jesus . . . yet, it was at that moment that I, too, felt loved. I felt that God was blessing *me* for answering an inner call to be baptised. As understanding dawned, I fell to my knees in praise – for I realised that it had been God who had drawn me to the water's edge – it was *he* who had led me to be baptised. It is God who has altered the course of my life.

As I recall that voice of thunder and the words, 'This is my son, whom I love', I smile – for I know that I, too, belong to God . . . that he loves me also . . . and I know that I love God – the joy in my heart confirms it.

A Prayer

Thank you for the thunder, Lord, and for your words of love. Keep me always listening to your voice, that I may learn to discern it – and respond. Amen.

Jesus Heals a Leper
Mark 1:40-45

The disease was awful and the stench of my own rotting body lived with me day and night. I felt ashamed and unclean – so I lived alone, wouldn't even join a colony . . . I *couldn't*, not the way I was.

Then Jesus came by. I knew it was him by the crowds who followed him. I'd heard that he taught love and forgiveness . . . I'd heard tales of how he had sent away demons – *and* healed the sick.

I thought, 'He won't want to come near me – not as I am, for the whole of me . . . *stinks*.'

So, I hid. I hid behind the rocks and watched as he came nearer.

Jesus *couldn't* have known I was there – could he? Yet, he seemed to look straight towards me . . . as if he were searching for me . . . as if he were heading in my direction for a purpose.

With horror, I realised that Jesus had come *so* close to me – and I was going to allow him to walk away. My one chance of healing was within reach, and I had chosen to hide. At that moment, I recognised that stupid pride – and the fear of rejection – was keeping me behind the rock.

JESUS HEALS A LEPER

Like a child playing hide-and-seek, I knew I was being sought and . . . oh, how I *wanted* to be found! So I gave myself up!

Struggling to reach him, and aware of the stench which still clung to me, I fell to my knees crying, 'Jesus, Jesus, please make me whole.' I indicated the mess I was in and pleaded: 'You can make me clean . . . if you are willing.'

Jesus looked at me . . . he stretched out his hands to me, and rested them on my shoulders. 'I *am* willing.' That's what he said to me.

Jesus was willing to make me whole . . . to risk touching something vile. Jesus touched me . . . and made me clean.

As I look back on that day, I remember his look of undisguised delight as I emerged from my place of hiding. Jesus *knew* where I was, but he gave me the choice of decision: to face him and be healed – or not.

Now, if anyone asks me to speak of that time, if I am willing to recount my story – I think of a gentle touch on my shoulders and I see a kindly, loving face above mine . . . and without hesitation, in the name of Jesus, I repeat his words . . . 'I *am* willing.'

A Prayer

Heal me, Lord, as I emerge from my own place of hiding – and thank you for being so very willing to cleanse and heal me. Amen.

The Road to Emmaus
Luke 24:13-35

We walked in misery along our desert road. With grief in our hearts, we discussed the death of our Teacher, and wondered how we would survive without him – for we had lost everything.

A stranger joined us and started speaking to us. We jumped in surprise, for neither of us had heard his footsteps on the path behind us. He asked what was wrong and why were we so sad? Amazed at his ignorance, we stared at him . . . where could he have been that he had not heard that Jesus, the Messiah, had been crucified . . . murdered . . . and that now even his body was missing.

We had judged too soon, for as we walked, the stranger began to explain the scriptures to us . . . he was a *fascinating* man – so interesting – and knowledgeable. It was the two of us who had been ignorant . . . and blind.

We enjoyed his company and were surprised to see that we had reached the village so quickly. This man had walked the length of the desert road with us – somehow, he had reached the raw pain in our hearts . . . and the heavy weight of grief, which we knew at the start of our journey, had lifted!

We *couldn't* let him walk on alone – it was getting dark – and we were delighted when he agreed to stay and share our supper of bread and cheese.

THE ROAD TO EMMAUS

It was when he broke the bread . . . the *way* he broke it . . . that we realised who had been walking alongside us . . . Jesus! Our own, dear Jesus.

As the joy of recognition leapt in my heart, I saw love dancing in the eyes of Jesus. But as I stretched out my hands to him, as I stepped forwards to reach him, he vanished . . . gone, as silently as he came. But he left the bread, still broken, behind.

Dazed, we looked at each other, then with a leap into the air we shouted out our joy – we had *seen* Jesus, we had *talked* to him. How fast we ran to reach you all – how much lighter our steps were as we shared our delight.

We had begun our journey not knowing how to survive . . . now we're back, telling you the good news that Jesus *is* alive . . . come, look at this bread, see how it is broken and so, let us rejoice together and eat that which Jesus himself broke . . . for us to share.

A Prayer

Lord Jesus, you walk with us in our desert places, yet often we miss your presence. Keep us always faithful in the knowledge that you *are* with us – and that we will find you in the breaking of the bread – always. Amen.

The Centurion and His Servant
Matthew 8:5-13

Unable to move, my servant had looked at me with despair and fear – he knew he was dying. We all knew. I read the plea for help in his eyes . . . but I could do nothing – except sit and wait with him.

I closed my eyes and asked God for guidance and as I sat, waiting, a thought came gently into my mind – go and find Jesus – tell *him*. With a smile of hope, I left my servant and headed for the door.

I found Jesus just entering our town and, with a great sense of urgency, I ran to him.

As I reached his side, my anxiety fell away . . . a peace, total and complete, settled within me and I knew with a certainty that all would now be well.

Jesus listened while I told him about my servant – that he was dying, and that he was special to me. Gently, he took my arm and turned me around to face home . . . he offered to come with me . . . to cure him.

With all my heart, I believed in Jesus . . . I had heard his teachings, knew of his healing ministry . . . his miracles. Jesus, who had command over storms and seas, demons –

THE CENTURION AND HIS SERVANT

and even death itself – was prepared to come to the home of a Roman officer.

In great humility, I looked at him and said, 'Lord, just say the word and my servant will be healed.'

. . . I, a soldier, used to ordering people to do my bidding – and trusting that things would be done – had asked Jesus, with the same unshakeable trust, to order the invisible – to do the impossible. And he did.

A Prayer

Keep me trusting, Lord, that *nothing* is invisible – or impossible – for you. Amen.

Jesus Feeds the Five Thousand
Luke 9:12-17

Five loaves and two fish, that's all he had – and there were thousands of us to feed! I watched him break the first loaf and tear it into pieces – he gave it out for distribution and started on the next, and then the next . . . then the fish . . . then more bread.

The fish was good – it added flavour to our meal. Our group shared out our portion with others – and they, in turn, shared theirs with us . . . and as I ate, I watched Jesus – still breaking the bread, still content to stand with us, feeding us, sharing everything he had with us. Jesus performed a miracle, right in front of my very own eyes, for those loaves and fishes fed each and every one of us – with plenty left over.

As my mind looks back on that day, I remember Jesus' words: 'Gather up the fragments so that *nothing* may be lost.' Many of us helped to pick up the pieces – to clear up the mess – we filled up the baskets and gave them back to Jesus.

I followed Jesus – to the end. And it is only now, so much later, that my eyes have been opened to his message of that day . . . for as I envisage those five loaves and two fish, I see that, *unbroken*, they could never have fed us all. No. In order to feed us, those perfectly intact, whole pieces *had* to be broken – for it was in their brokenness that they reached us . . . and fed us.

JESUS FEEDS THE FIVE THOUSAND

In time our groups split up, drifting away in twos and threes ... I see now that we, too, needed to be broken apart so that each and every one of us could reach other travellers and tell them the good news of Jesus.

And see, here, in my basket, I carry one small loaf and one small fish, so that I may share them on my journey – and, so far, I have always had just about enough.

A Prayer

Gather me up, Lord Jesus, into your basket of love. Take all my brokenness and make of me what you will. Keep my eyes open, dear Lord, that I may find others and place them, in turn, in your basket – that *none* may be lost. Amen.

Judas Iscariot
Matthew 27:3-5

I hadn't meant for him to die . . . dear God . . . not *that* . . . I didn't mean to betray him . . . really, I didn't. I thought he'd escape – that he'd perform a miracle – prove he was God's Son . . . He could have done that and made himself King . . . but Jesus just stood there – and called me friend.

What have I done, dear God? . . . What *have* I done?

With a sickening feeling I followed the crowd as they took him away – for I knew that my own foolish, arrogant, frustrated pride had led Jesus . . . and me . . . to this. I felt as if a knife had pierced my heart – I wish it had, for I realised that whether or not I had meant it, I had instigated Jesus' arrest.

I tried to get him back – told them that I had not intended for him to die, that Jesus was innocent – the Son of God – that he was too good, too kind, too loved to be killed. But they wouldn't listen.

I tried to give the money back – but they wouldn't take it. They laughed and gave me a new name . . . Betrayer of Friends . . . and that is what I am. For I have betrayed Jesus, and sent him to his death on a cross . . .

In desolation I have sat in this tree, knowing that I cannot live with what I have done. And so, as I feel the stranglehold of the rope around my neck, I jump . . . and cry out, 'I'm sorry . . . dear God . . . forgive.'

A Prayer

Father God, I make mistakes, and mess things up – I see my errors and then regret them. Thank you for your forgiving love, and for the fact that I need only cry, 'Dear God . . . forgive' . . . and you do. Amen.

Martha and Mary
Luke 10:38-42

Sometimes I feel defeated, Lord – when I look at my schedule and the time left in which to do it all. So I come to you and lay my burden down at your feet . . . and you take it from me . . . then I pick it all up and start running again!

> *The Reply*
>
> Child, you make me laugh. I watch you scurrying around, desperately trying to complete all these self-made tasks – yes, self-made . . . for *you* accepted these jobs . . . you even took on others' responsibilities.
>
> That's the Martha in you, child, and I love you dearly for it – but now, come, sit here in my peace and allow the Mary in you to just rest and be. For without Mary, you cannot exist . . . you will not learn to grow or discern my voice when I call to you.
>
> Be still, child, for you will find that when Mary is fulfilled, she will energise Martha – and so the work will be completed more effectively and you will feel at one with yourself and back in harmony with life.

A Prayer

Lord Jesus, you always seem to *know*! Keep me faithful to both the Mary and the Martha in me, so that I may sit at your feet in peace. Amen.

Mary Magdalene

It was a special love between him and me . . . all embracing, all empowering . . . a deep, peaceful love.

We had a special friendship, Jesus and I . . . we shared trust and understanding . . .

Laughed and cried – together . . . he knew my worst side . . . and that's all right, between friends.

His hug was special as we said goodbye . . . our tears swapped faces as for one, brief moment I felt his lips against my skin – and he felt mine on his . . . the day before he died.

Our meeting outside the tomb was special . . . as he watched my wretchedness – and then my gladness. His voice was special as he spoke my name: 'Mary.'

I am special, for he chose me . . . to see him first. He chose to speak to *me* at the open tomb. He trusted me to tell the others – that he will come, and to tell them to be prepared for his call on that day.

A Prayer

Lord Jesus, thank you for your love and friendship, and for making me special to you. Keep me ever ready, that I may hear your voice – and then respond. Amen.

Jesus Washes the Disciples' Feet
John 13:1-10

I didn't want him to wash my feet! But when he did, I felt such humility . . . so humble . . . such a oneness with him. You should have seen the dirt that he washed away! Mud and grime, gently eased away by his soft, loving touch . . . I could have washed *his* feet . . . why didn't I do that? His hour had come – he'd told us that – so, why didn't I show *my* love for *him*?

It would have been so easy – everything was there: water, bowl, towel . . . Jesus . . . he was there too – *then*. He was right in front of me – why didn't I kneel before him and offer myself to him? A lost opportunity – as the next day, he was gone.

Jesus, my friend, did you see the love I had for you? Through my over-zealous, over-loud, exuberant personality . . . did you *see* how I loved you? I took it all for granted – our time together – the fun, the tears . . . I wish I had done more for you, listened more attentively. More lost opportunities – I miss you.

> *Jesus' Reply*
>
> My very special friend, your eyes showed me your love and I love you just as you are. I *wanted* to

wash your feet. I wanted to show my love for you all. I knew your paths would not be easy as you followed me. I could find no better way of showing my deep sorrow at leaving you – my deep honour in serving you all – in private – one more time. My friend, you did not lose the opportunity, you took it – by allowing me to serve you, to show my love for you, to teach you. You *are* following my example . . . you are serving others . . . all is not lost.

A Prayer

Lord Jesus, help me to be more attentive to others, to serve them, to wash *their* feet: Lord, show me the opportunities – and let me not waste them. Amen.

Jesus Appears to the Disciples
John 21:1-14

The Sea of Tiberius

We thought our night had been wasted. We'd caught nothing . . . done nothing. It seemed that, without our Lord's presence, we couldn't even catch fish any more. Shoulders slumped, and feeling miserable, we gave up our night's futile efforts and headed for land. Then we saw him . . . heard his dear voice calling to us – giving instructions – showing us where the fish were . . . our friend Jesus . . . still showing us the way. He gave us our whole night's work in a few minutes.

It was here that he stood, this very spot, just stood – waiting for us. His feast already prepared, ready for us to taste and eat as we reached the shore. My heart had skipped a beat when I realised it really *was* Jesus, watching patiently – and I still at sea with the others. The boat seemed to take for ever to get in to the shallows, so that I could step out and wade ashore, and see the sparkle in his eyes as we shared in the joy of companionship – one more time.

No meal will ever be the same, for we tasted joy and happiness, exchanged laughter and love. A deep, deep peace settled between us – on the edge of this shore. And as I stand here now, I *still* feel the love between us . . . I hear the echo of his laughter and I wonder . . . how *did* Jesus find those fish he'd cooked – when they were deep-sea fish and so hard to find?

A Prayer

Lord Jesus, you stand at the shoreline of my life with patience. Give me the eyes to see you, the ears to hear you, and the heart to obey you – with joy and love. Amen.

Return of the Prodigal Son
Luke 15:11-32

It's always been so comfortable here. Yes, we'd had to work for you, but food was always on the table, clothes were always cleaned, there was always a bed to lie on. When I left – with all my inheritance – well, I was OK!

I didn't think . . .

I just left, pockets bulging, shoes on my feet – it was me for the high life – and I had it all. I was the most popular person around.

Only it wasn't *me* who was so popular – it was my money.

What a leveller . . . to find that my pockets were running empty, to find that my high life was, in fact, the low life!

And then, feeding the pigs! Starving as I was, I realised the pigs at least were pleased to see me, they relied on me. They used to nudge at my legs and snort gently – as if they were thanking me for my care of them – and I – all too ready to steal food from them and spoil their trust in me.

It was then that I realised how I had spoiled *your* trust in me. The truth hit hard. I had wasted your precious gifts to me. I had thrown away my inheritance – that of your love for me.

I had thrown away *you*. *I* had done that! But you once said, 'There is a way back for everyone.'

A Prayer

Father, I kneel before you, shattered at my brokenness, ashamed of what I have thrown away, stunned at my stupidity. I kneel before you – as I am now – a poor, footsore, weary traveller who has strayed from the path and who longs to find a sure foothold again. Lord, please forgive.

The Reply

My son, I watched you from afar, I watched your back disappear – straight, strong, bold and useless to me. I watched you from afar, I saw your return – thin, weary, bent, starving – and humbled.
Come to me, my child, there is a wisdom of understanding in you now and *that* I can use. You are mine, you always were – I loved you all the while. Come, tell me about the pigs; for it is they who brought you home to me.

A Prayer

Father God, thank you for your unconditional love for me – even through the wild times. Father, your strength fills my weakness. Please show me the way – your way – I am weary of my own road. Amen.

www.ingramcontent.com/pod-product-compliance
Lightning Source LLC
Chambersburg PA
CBHW060459080526
44584CB00015B/1487